THE DISCOVERY: EXPLORE OUTER SPACE & THE SOLAR SYSTEM

Written by Jimmy Nightingale -- Illustrated by Grace Ji

This Book Belongs to:

_____

Copyright (c) 2020 Jimmy Nightingale and Big Barn Press

THE DISCOVER CATS EXPLORE OUTER SPACE

WRITTEN BY JIMMY NIGHTINGALE   ILLUSTRATED BY GRACE JI

Cornelius would have lessons about all sorts of topics, industries, and fields, and this time, he wanted to teach them about one of his favorite topics: outer space and the solar system that we live in.

For this lesson, Cornelius had secured a top secret spaceship that would allow the three cats to blast off into space. He made sure Ginny and Max had their helmets and seatbelts on, and got ready for blast off.

5...4...3...2...1... GO!

"What's gravity?" "Gravity is an invisible force that causes things to move toward each other. Even you and Max have gravity! The greater the size, the greater the gravity, and that's why we need to go so fast to blast into space!"

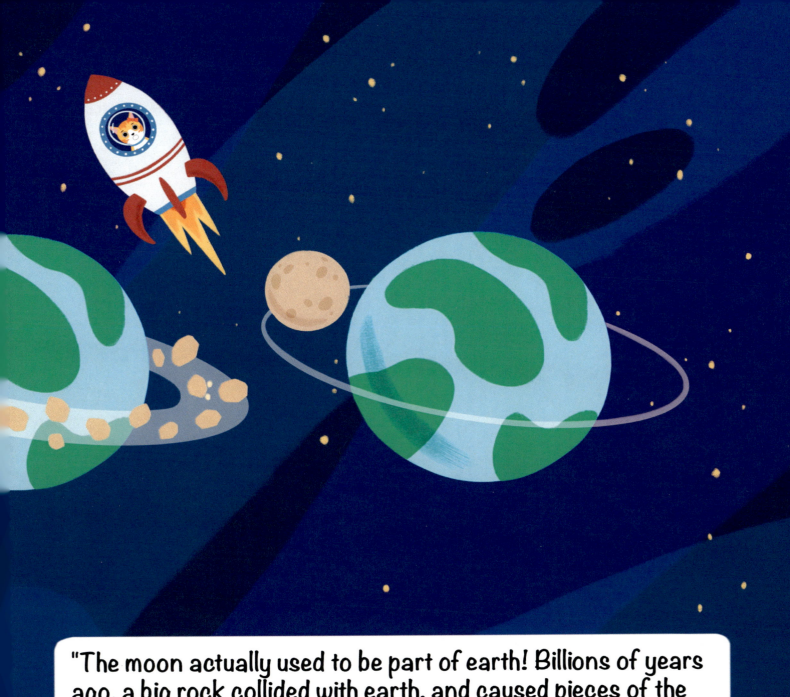

"The moon actually used to be part of earth! Billions of years ago, a big rock collided with earth, and caused pieces of the earth to break off. Eventually, those pieces became the moon."

"And it's so hot in there, too. The surface temperature of the sun is 27 million degrees Fahrenheit. No wonder we get sunburns!"

Some are big (Jupiter). Some are small (Pluto).

Some are hot (Venus).

Some are cold (Neptune).

Some are slow (Venus).

Some are fast (Mercury).

Some have rings (Saturn).

Some don't (Mars).

And one is even sideways (Uranus).

It was time to go farther! Cornelius sped up and headed past Pluto, the farthest and smallest planet from the sun.

Along the way, he saw something shiny in the distance, and became very excited.

"But what's even cooler is that there is a Golden Record on Voyager, which is information about us for any aliens that might see it!"

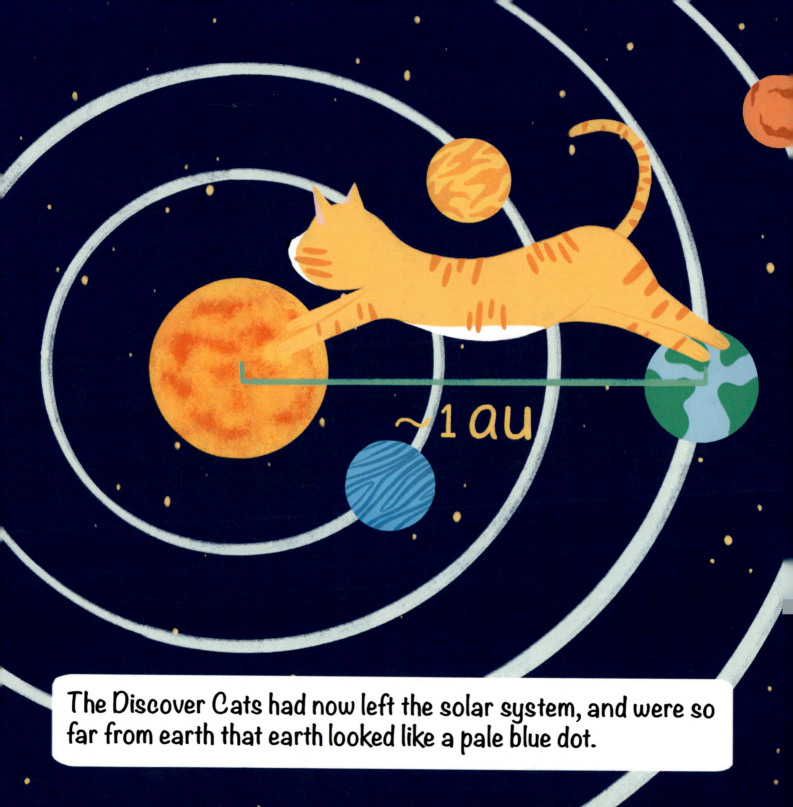

In fact, they were so far that it didn't make sense to use miles anymore. Cornelius said, "When we talk about distances in space, we use AU, which is the distance from earth to the sun. We are about 45 AU from home right now!"

Ginny and Max got a little bit scared, "That sounds so far! I can't believe it! It takes us 20 minutes just to walk to school!"

Made in the USA
Middletown, DE
16 December 2020